The 44th Year

Emerald Hallman

Presentation by *BookLeaf Publishing*

Web: www.bookleafpub.com

E-mail: info@bookleafpub.com

ISBN: 9789357742672

First edition 2023

I dedicate this book to God and myself because I really had to learn and appreciate the God given strength that I had to get through this more mentally and emotionally than physically. There was no one holding my hand in the darkest times, there was just God and that was MORE THAN I needed.

ACKNOWLEDGEMENT

It's funny, when you're going through something so life changing you expect to be able to count on the people who are "closest to you" and it's amazing and sad to find out that they are the ones who will be the most far away...I would like to acknowledge and thank the people who WERE there-in ways that I couldn't fathom they would be. So with my whole heart and soul let me say to Aries, Lisa, Aida and my beautiful and special Ava thank you so much for going above and beyond to help me in any and EVERY way. You four helped me more than I can ever explain and I am eternally grateful to you all.

PREFACE

This book found me and not the other way around. I was (and currently still am as I write this) going through chemotherapy treatment for breast cancer. I happened to stumble upon an ad on social media for writing 21 poems in 21 days. Now, at the time I was in a rough place mentally, of course physically but mostly emotionally and I didn't have an outlet for all of these feelings.

To be honest, I was kinda drowning and slipping into depression...I felt like I needed to do something-ANYTHING to steer me away from that. I found this to be a challenge and at the very least a much needed distraction. Also, I found it to be an outlet because that's something I didn't feel I had. And so, here we are. Just me expressing myself and hoping maybe to be of service to someone else reading this and possibly having a hard time in life as well. And if so, then I'm ok with that and thank you for taking the time to care enough to read.

August

"What a difference a day makes"... isn't that how the saying goes?
Because one day I was completely fine and the next I wasn't.
I had no idea what what I was in for
Nor was I prepared...would I ever be?

44

I've been waiting for you.
I've been hiding from you.
I've been expecting you.
I've been running from you.
Because I knew that when you came,
Nothing would ever be the same.
And oh man was I right
Because in just one night
You completely changed my life
The prophecy came true
In every way through and through
And now I'm left here with you...44

The Port

3

I can't sleep, anxiety is taking over.
Did I think it through?
Is this the best choice?
My poor frail veins can't take much more
Tissue corroding, nerves exploding...with pain.
It's a simple procedure-one incision.
Don't worry this is the best decision-trust
yourself.

The Happy Parts

I put my Christmas tree up in November
And then I got the news.
I plugged it everyday in December
And then I got the blues.
Because I realized that soon
That happy part of me,
Would be gone like the moon
 On the day I'd take down the tree.
But I just couldn't do it
Because I needed those lights
To remind me of the happy parts
On these long, sleepless nights.
So I'll leave it up a few months more
To give me solace through the Winter
Til' Spring is at my door.
And the sun shines on my face
Bringing joy back to my heart
And I'll smell the new fresh flowers
And feel new happy parts.

I Am Here

5

Some days I can't rest
But I am here.
Some days I can't stop crying
But I am here.
Some days I feel depressed
But I am here.
Some days I feel like dying
But I am STILL HERE!

Aida

I have a friend, a beautiful soul
She makes me smile when I'm blue.
We talk, we laugh, sometimes we cry
One thing I have found to be true.
No matter how bad or low we may feel
Through some of the days that we lead
We greet once a week & after we speak
We feel a lot better indeed!

The Red Devil

I went to war with the Red Devil
Unsure if I could win.
To be honest, I was doubtful
My faith was low within.
See I'd heard about this devil
And I knew he was no joke.
An opponent hard to beat
Who left most who tried to-broke.

Today

I woke up today smiling and happy
remembering I'm blessed
Not angry or in pain or feeling depressed
And yes, I'm still behind in bills
but I didn't feel the stress
I talked to my babies in the phone
for awhile
Ava being Ava did her usual and
made me smile
I didn't think about the next treatment
or how many I have left
Or feel my lump to see if it shrunk
or worry about death
I just enjoyed the day in every way
with every breath

Fill The Cup

9

I love you-let me start there.
Not "I love you more than...or because of...or
regardless..." Just I love you.
I haven't told you in that form-the most simplest,
purest and HONEST form. Somewhere along
the way, I forgot to remind you that you, me-I
COME FIRST. I just have to remind myself that
I am deserving of this love. I will no longer give
it to someone who does not want it or won't
accept it. It's time to pour into my own cup
because if I don't...who will?

Time

I've taken you for granted constantly
The ultimate procrastinator.
Don't worry I've got it all planned out
Relax, I'll do it later.
And even as I write these words
At the eleventh hour,
It seems I haven't changed a bit
With these "last minute" powers!

Alone

I've been alone most of my life
Not outwardly, but mostly inward
Never really felt stable or like I belonged
Or fit in-at least not for long
Or supported, or a part of, like a real
Part of ANYTHING
Always moving, changing schools, or families,
or friends
No tree, no roots, no one....

Weak

I'm coming more to terms
with myself these days
I always felt weak for crying....
Weird for feeling-my feelings and others
Not being able to hold back tears
Or not feel other's pain
I hated it, it felt like a weakness,
 made me an easy target
Even accused of faking it,
not being genuine
You really think I want to cry this easily?
To look weak and crazy, not being able to
explain why it hurts so bad?
It's not even my pain sometimes but I swear it
feels like it is....

F

13

Forget fear. Keep hope. Enjoy every moment and appreciate life.

I

14

Ignite the fire within. Never lose who you are.
Stay warm and stay bright!

G

15

God is within. God has me always. Never forget.
With him I can't lose. Pray, believe and
maintain.

H

Hello world! When this is all done and my strength is renewed I will make sure to see as much of this world as I am blessed to!

T

Tough as nails, hard as rocks, soft as silk, strong as locks...me

Grace

God gives us grace each and everyday and a will
to live and a mouth to pray and a heart to love
and a mind to think and of course a life with
which to live!!!!